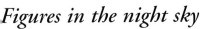

Drawing a star

There are many ways to draw stars. Here are several basic designs with which to start.

Figures in the night sky

In ancient times people tried to find the forms of mythological beings or the shapes of animals in the groupings of the stars. By examining the shapes of the constellations we can discover the animal and human forms of the classical period.

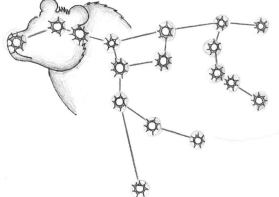

The constellation of the giant Orion. If we look carefully, we can find the figure of this mythical character in the arrangement of the stars.

In the constellation of the Dragon the distribution of the stars can be taken to form the shape of a dragon.

To practice, copy a constellation onto paper and try to determine which figure it represents.

This is how the animal that gives its name to the constellation of the Great Bear is formed within its grouping of stars.

FIELD GUIDES

The Night Sky

Text by
Eduardo
Banqueri

First American Edition published in 2007 by
Enchanted Lion Books, 45 Main Street, Suite 519
Brooklyn, NY 11201

© 2006 Parramón Ediciones, S.A
Translation © 2006 Parramón Ediciones, S.A.

Conception and realization
Parramón Ediciones, S.A.

Editor
Lluís Borràs

Assistant Editor
Cristina Vilella

Text
Eduardo Banqueri

Graphic design and layout
Estudi Toni Inglès

Photography
AGE-Fotostock, NASA (GSA), NASA (JPL),
NASA (JSC), Prisma, J. Vidal

Illustrations
Studio Marcel Socias
Gabi Martin (endpapers)

Director of Production
Rafael Marfil

Production
Manel Sánchez

Preprinting
Pacmer, S.A.

For information about permissions to reproduce selections from this
book, write to Permissions, Enchanted Lion Books, 45 Main Street,
Suite 519, Brooklyn, NY 11201

A CIP record is on file with the Library of Congress

ISBN-13: 978-1-59270-066-0
ISBN-10: 1-59270-066-7

Printed in Spain

2 4 6 8 10 9 7 5 3 1

CONTENTS

4 EXPLORING THE SKY

Beyond the clouds

6 THE TELESCOPE

How close they are!

8 THE PLANISPHERE

A map of the sky

10 THE GALAXIES

Islands in space

12 THE STARS

The energy of the universe

14 THE TERRESTRIAL PLANETS

Our neighbors

16 THE JOVIAN PLANETS

Far from the sun

18 THE SUN

Spying on the star king

20 THE MOON

Beautiful Selene

22 ECLIPSES

A grand spectacle

24 THE CONSTELLATIONS

Figures in the firmament

26 THE SKY IN THE SOUTHERN HEMISPHE

More fantastic figures

28 COMETS, STARS AND METEORITES

The rascals of space

30 THE ASTRONOMICAL OBSERVATORY

Scanning the universe

32 NEBULAS, GALAXIES, STARS, SHOWERS

A Universe of Wonders

The aim of this Field Guide is to serve as a handy tool for observing the night sky, helping to bring us closer to the amazing world of comets, meteors, asteroids, planets, stars, galaxies and other phenomena in the universe. In addition, it provides simple advice on how to use binoculars and telescopes and shows us what an astronomical research observatory is like.

To begin to know the night sky, we need only take time to look. In addition to familiarizing ourselves with the sky, the study of star atlases will help us to locate constellations, stars and planets. Having done this, the use of binoculars will make it possible to perceive double stars, variable stars, nebulas, star clusters, some galaxies and details of the moon.

If a strong interest develops in the night sky as it is explored, the next step would be to try out a telescope. Although setting it up and handling it are a little more complicated than using binoculars, it allows us to begin to discover what our eyes alone cannot—the fascinating secrets of the universe.

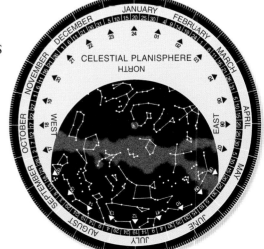

Beyond the Clouds

To begin to learn about the universe, the first thing is to look up at the sky both during the day and at night, though it is at night that the sky is most striking. In the daytime, only the sun can be seen regularly, with the moon visible only occasionally, and the appearance of other phenomena, such as Venus or Mercury, a rare event.

compass
serves to determine direction and to orient the planisphere

planisphere
used to locate the constellations and bright stars

binoculars
allow us to see more than 43,000 stars and to observe the moon, with its mountains and craters, as well as star clusters, nebulas and galaxies.

Observing the sky at night

1. If possible, try to go stargazing with someone knowledgeable.

2. Dress appropriately for the time of year.

3. Look for a place away from city lights.

4. Avoid nights around the full moon, because its bright light will make for poor viewing.

5. Consult weather information to avoid running into cloudy skies or rain.

6. Take the time of year and the instruments available into consideration, preparing a list of the specific observations you would most like to make.

To observe the sky you must have the appropriate instruments. You also will need to consult the atlases and planispheres that correspond to the time of year.

First, binoculars

Unlike telescopes, binoculars are quite easy to use since they provide a more extensive visual field that is not inverted. In addition, they offer images that, in general, are much more luminous, making them particularly good for starting to observe the night sky.

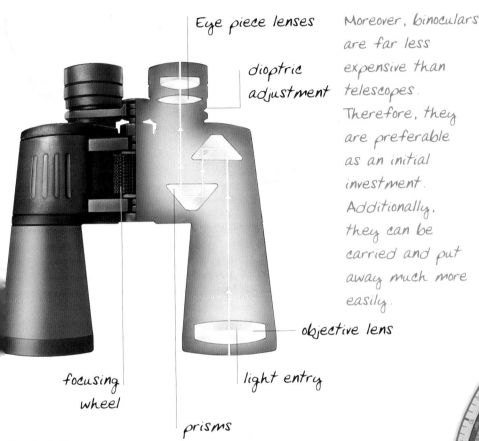

Eye piece lenses

dioptric adjustment

objective lens

focusing wheel

light entry

prisms

Moreover, binoculars are far less expensive than telescopes. Therefore, they are preferable as an initial investment. Additionally, they can be carried and put away much more easily.

flashlight
covered with red cellophane to look at star atlases and avoid dazzling the eyes; though it may not seem like it, the eye takes from 15 to 30 minutes to adjust to darkness.

observation notebook
for noting down the location of an object, the time, place, date, and conditions of observation, and for making simple diagrams to help in locating an object in future observations.

Where to find out more?

Astronomical societies and associations are non-profit organizations concerned with providing information about research and advances having to do with astronomy and related sciences. These organizations are open to anyone and are a good place to start should a strong interest develop.

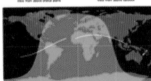

The Internet can also be consulted for information, with some things, such as a satellite schedule for your specific area, easily tracked down.

The planisphere, or star atlas, shows us which celestial objects can be seen and which will be hidden from our sight at every hour of the day, every day of the year.

5

How Close They Are!

The telescope is an instrument that makes it possible to see distant objects by taking in more light and enlarging the image obtained. It is made up of a pair of lenses, one of which is called objective, because it is closer to the object, and another called the eyepiece, since it is closer to the eyes.

Refractor telescope

This is ideal for the observation of planets and visible double stars, since its aperture is not very large and its focal length is considerable. It has a superior optic quality and excellent definition. High quality refractor telescopes are quite expensive, though ordinary, more affordable ones can also be obtained.

Reflector telescope

This is the most commonly used telescope among amateurs thanks to its good quality and reasonable price. The eyepiece of these telescopes is on one side and on the front part of the tube. Their chief advantage is their great capacity for taking in light, so they are ideal for the observation of objects with a low level of luminosity (nebulas, galaxies, star clusters and other deep space objects).

Hunting a celestial body

When searching for a celestial body, an eyepiece of low magnification, capable of taking in a great extension of sky, should be used as it provides a view of the weaker celestial bodies. Once we have focused on the field of a specific celestial body, we can change to a more powerful eyepiece, being careful not to move the telescop

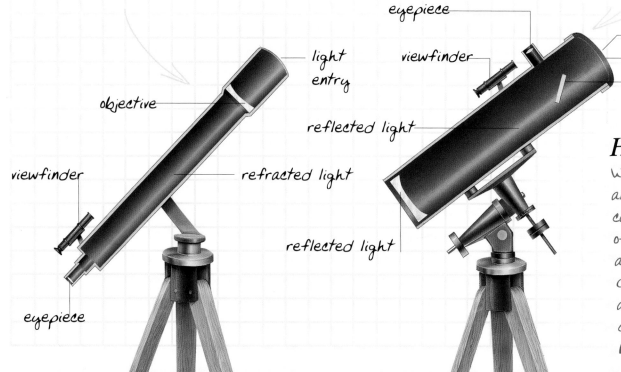

objective

viewfinder

eyepiece

light entry

refracted light

reflected light

eyepiece

viewfinder

reflected light

light entry

objective

secondary reflector

If the Earth moves, the telescope does too

For the human eye the rotation of the sky is very slow, too slow, in fact, to perceive. A telescope, however, greatly multiplies the speed of rotation, so that any star observed with it moves swiftly toward the edge of our field of vision and then disappears, unless we continually adjust the direction of the telescope. This adjustment can be made using two types of mounting that make it possible to counteract the turning of the Earth and thus follow the apparent movement of the stars: azimuth mounting and equatorial mounting.

The viewfinder

This is a small, low-power telescope attached to a main instrument that helps to direct it by obtaining an initial view of the area under observation.

Unlike binoculars, all telescopes produce images that are upside down.

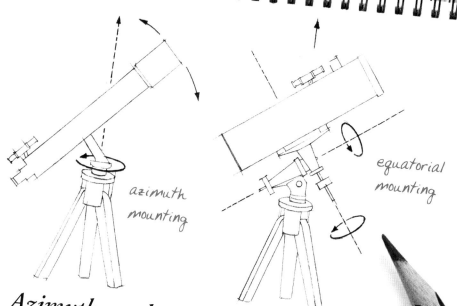

azimuth mounting

equatorial mounting

Azimuth or altazimuth mounting

This makes it possible to move a telescope both horizontally and vertically. While it is simpler than equatorial mounting, it is more difficult to handle when moving a telescope in a way that is synchronized with the Earth's rotation in order to compensate for the movement of celestial objects throughout the night. Therefore, this is not the best instrument for astronomical observation since the two axes have to be moved constantly to follow the movements of a star.

Equatorial mounting

This makes it possible to move a telescope sideways with a single movement so that it is much easier to synchronize the telescope with the rotation of the Earth, thus compensating for the movement of objects in the sky throughout the night.

7

A Map of the Sky

A planisphere represents the celestial sphere on a flat surface. Its origin is very ancient, and its use is based on the false belief that the Earth is at the center of the universe and that it is the vault of the heavens that spins around us. A planisphere tells us which celestial objects can be seen in the sky and which are hidden from our sight at every hour of the day for every day of the year.

Using the planisphere

A planisphere works with sun time. Remember that in some countries in summer the clock is set two hours ahead of sun time and in the winter one hour ahead.

1. Turn the movable disk until the hour of observation coincides with the date.

2. Hold the planisphere over your head with the N of the planisphere toward the north. The part of the map that is inside the ellipse of the horizon is the part that will be visible to you.

circular scale with hours of the day (0-24)

the direction of the compass, north, is indicated on its face

circular scale that divides the sky of the planisphere into 360°

circular scale with the months of the year

circular scale with the days of each month

the Milky Way is marked in light blue

a central area (inside the circle of the days) where stars appear

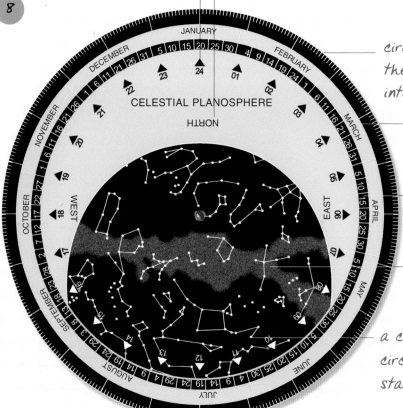

A planisphere is composed of two parts, one of which turns on top of the other. The top disk has a transparent window that corresponds to the visible part of the sky. The rest of the sky is not visible, since at the date and time indicated it is hidden below the horizon.

Intruders

On a planisphere, only the stars that are visible are represented. The planets that can be seen (Mercury, Venus, Mars, Jupiter and Saturn) are not represented, nor are the sun and moon. Thus, if we see a bright star that does not appear on the planisphere it is probably a planet.

By keeping the shutter of a 35 mm or digital camera open, we can take a long exposure picture of the night sky. The streaks of light appearing over the picture reflect the movement of the stars that occurs as a result of the Earth's rotation.

Far out above our heads, the night sky appears to be a vast expanse dotted by unmoving stars, when in fact these stars move second to second, from east to west.

A planisphere is centered on the North or Pole Star and represents on its surface all of the stars that are visible throughout the year. The edge of the disk usually coincides with the celestial equator, but it is common for stars situated a few degrees further to the south to be represented as well.

Projection of the northern hemisphere

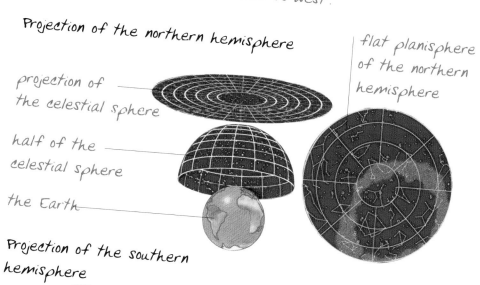

projection of the celestial sphere

half of the celestial sphere

the Earth

flat planisphere of the northern hemisphere

Projection of the southern hemisphere

flat planisphere of the southern hemisphere

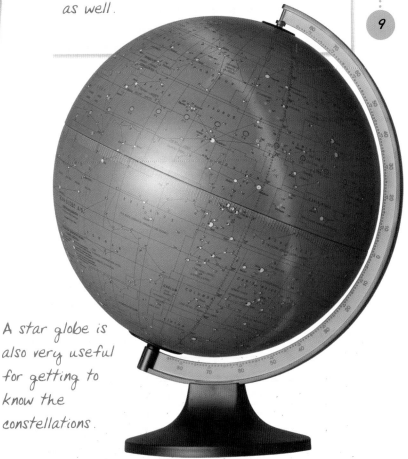

A star globe is also very useful for getting to know the constellations.

Islands in Space

A galaxy is a gigantic collection of millions or billions of stars, planets, gas and dust that is held together by gravity. Galaxies are the most impressive celestial objects in the universe. There are hundreds of billions of them, forming genuine islands of matter in space.

The Milky Way

This is a spiral galaxy made up of hundreds of billions of stars, among them our sun. For an observer on Earth, the Milky Way looks like a dimly luminous band stretching across the night sky. It is most visible on clear, moonless summer nights.

our solar system
this is in the outer reaches of the Milky Way galaxy. Almost everything we can see in the sky belongs to this galaxy.

galactic center
this is where most of the stars in the Milky Way are concentrated, which, along with those making up the halo, are the oldest in the galaxy

spiral arms
these turn slowly on an axis that runs through the galactic center in such a way that they trail along behind during rotation

galactic disk
this contains the young stars that whirl around the nucleus or galactic center of the galaxy

Globular clusters

These are densely packed balls that contain hundreds of thousands of very old stars. The globular clusters of our galaxy are dispersed along the spherical halo that surrounds it.

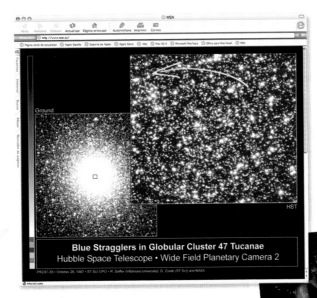

Blue Stragglers in Globular Cluster 47 Tucanae
Hubble Space Telescope • Wide Field Planetary Camera 2

Nebulas

These are enormous clouds of light interstellar gases (hydrogen, helium) and cosmic dust (carbon, iron, silicon). Due to the condensation and accumulation of matter that occur, these are also the places where solar systems like our own are formed.

Open clusters

These are groups of stars that are to be found within the galactic disk, which is where the stars themselves have recently been formed. These clusters contain young, hot stars.

— galactic halo
a spherical cloud that surrounds the galaxies and is made up of globular clusters and interstellar dust. It contains the oldest objects in our galaxy.

A Great variety of galaxies

Galaxies can take the form of either a globe or a lens. There also are galaxies that are flat, elliptical, spiral (like ours) or irregular in form. They can be enormous, like Andromeda, or small, like its neighbor M32.

spiral

barred spiral

elliptical

irregular

The Energy of the Universe

Stars are masses of different sorts of gases that give off light. They are found at very high temperatures since there are nuclear reactions within them. The source of energy in a star is the nuclear fusion of hydrogen, which produces helium. When the matter necessary to maintain these nuclear reactions is exhausted, a star can turn into a red giant, explode to form a nova or supernova, and finally transform into a white dwarf, a neutron star or a black hole.

Types of stars

Stars are classified according to their size as super giants, giants, medium stars, small stars and dwarves. Depending on their temperature (from hot to cold), they can be blue, white, yellow or red.

multiple stars

Many stars that appear to be a single point of light to the naked eye turn out to be made up of two or more stars very close to one another when viewed through a telescope

red dwarf

This is a type of star that is very abundant in the universe and is distinguished by its small size and low surface temperature.

white dwarf

This is produced by the death of a medium mass star, such as our sun.

White dwarves, along with red dwarves, are the most abundant stars in the universe.

red giant

This is a star that has reached an advanced stage in its life cycle and is running out of hydrogen. It is large in size and low in surface temperature.

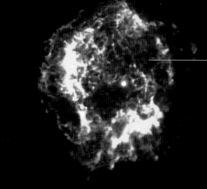

Variable brightness

There are a vast number of stars in the universe that do not project a constant amount of light over time, which means that their brightness varies. Many change in brightness periodically, while others do so in an irregular way, and a few do so explosively.

Alpha Cenauri is the star closest to the sun and is in the constellation Centaurus (The Centaur). In reality, it is a triple star, located 4.3 light years from Earth, visible only in the southern hemisphere. Alpha Centauri A, the closest of the three stars to the Earth, has a brightness equal to that of the sun.

Alpha Centauri

Jupiter

Moon

Venus

Mars

Betelgeuse (star)

Saturn

Mercury

Aldebaran (star)

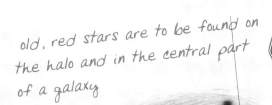

Centaurus A Nucleus
Hubble Space Telescope • WFPC2 • NICMOS
PRC98-14b • ST ScI OPO • May 14, 1998 • E. Schreier (ST ScI) and NASA

13

neutron star

this is one of the possible final objects produced by the explosion of a supernova

supernova

this results from the final explosion of a big star

Some little points of light

Except for the sun, we see stars at night as tiny points of light because they are at such an enormous distance from us. With the naked eye it is difficult to distinguish them from the planets close to the Earth.

old, red stars are to be found on the halo and in the central part of a galaxy

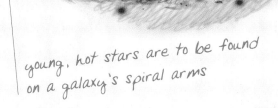

young, hot stars are to be found on a galaxy's spiral arms

Our Neighbors

Our solar system consists of a medium star that we call the sun and, as of August 2006, only eight planets—Mercury, Venus, Earth, Mars, Jupiter, Saturn, Uranus, and Neptune, with Pluto downgraded to a "dwarf planet," though this loss of status for Pluto remains contested and much debated. As for our eight planets, they divide into two groups, terrestrial and Jovian. The terrestrial planets—Mercury, Venus, Earth, and Mars—are those closest to the sun within our solar system and are so-named because like the Earth each has a compact, rocky surface.

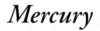

The probe, Venus Express.

Venus

Venus is the brightest object in the night sky after the moon, since it is the planet that is closest to the Earth. It shines most brightly at dawn and dusk. Using binoculars with a high level of magnification, we can observe that Venus has phases similar to those of the moon, since the sun lights only one of its sides.

14

Mars

Through a telescope, Mars appears to be a bright disk, deep orange in color. Each of its polar icecaps, which are white in color, are visible, as are its dark equatorial regions. Moreover, on its surface we can see variations of brightness depending on season and atmospheric conditions. Mars has two small satellites called Phobos and Deimos.

Mercury

To locate this planet it is important to keep in mind that it is always close to the horizon in the morning and at nightfall. Moreover, depending on the turbulence of the Earth's atmosphere, it appears as a point of varying brightness. With a telescope of 150 magnifications it appears to be half the moon's size when observed with the naked eye.

THE TERRESTRIAL PLANETS IN NUMBERS

	Mercury	Venus	Earth	Mars
Distance from sun (millions of miles)	43.4	67.5	92.9	141.6
Diameter (miles)	3,030	7522	7926	4217
Rotation around sun (days)	89,97 days	224,7 days	365,26 days	686,98 days
Orbital speed around sun	98 ft/s	71 ft/s	60 ft/s	45 ft/s
Rotation time	58 days 16 h.	243 days 14 m.	23 h. 56 m.	24 h. 37 m.
Mass (Earth = 1)	0.055	0.81	1	0.11
Density (water = 1))	5.43	5.25	5.52	3.95
Surface temperature (°F)	−292° to +806°	855°	−94° to +131°	−184° to +77°
Number of moons	–	–	1	2

One of the key factors that needs to be considered when observing the terrestrial planets is the distance between the sun and the planet. This distance is decisive since if it is very short, then the planet will be too close to the sun to be found and observed.

Venus is called "the morning star"

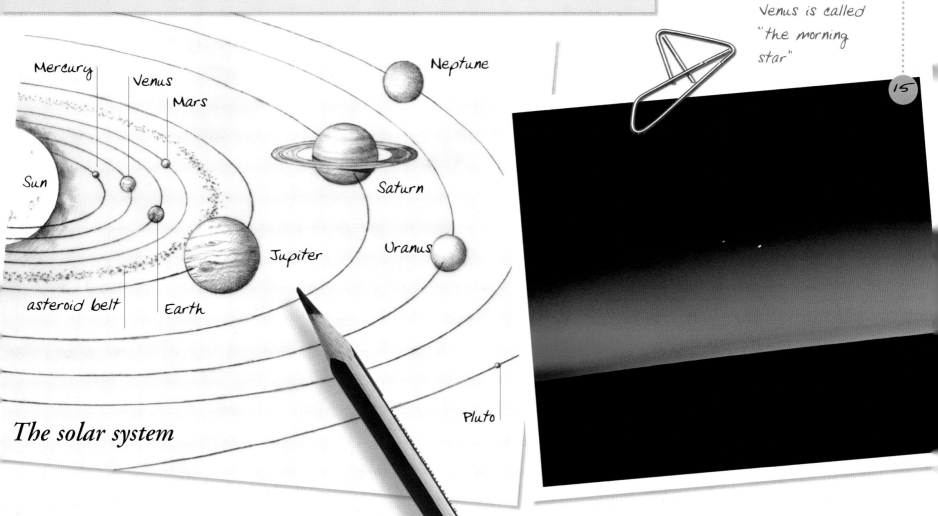

The solar system

15

Far from the Sun

The Jovian planets (the name refers to Jupiter), or giants, are quite a bit larger than the terrestrial planets and are far from the sun. This group includes Jupiter, Saturn, Uranus and Neptune. They are composed chiefly of hydrogen and helium in gaseous and liquid form. Pluto, the furthest from the sun, is not considered either terrestrial or Jovian, since it is composed of ice and rock. Hence, its new ranking as a dwarf planet.

Pluto

This is the smallest planet, or former planet, and the furthest from the sun. It is so far from the Earth and so small that its surface has never been observed from Earth and it has never been visited by a space probe. A telescope with an aperture of at least 200 mm is necessary in order to see it.

Neptune

Even when looked at through a telescope, Neptune can only be distinguished from nearby stars by its movement from one night to the next. Through bigger instruments, Neptune appears to be a bluish-green disk, little more than 2 inches in diameter.

THE JOVIAN PLANETS IN NUMBERS

	Jupiter	Saturn	Uranus	Neptune	Pluto
Distance from sun (millions of miles)	483.6	887.1	1784	2796.4	3667
Diameter (miles)	88,736	74,978	32.193	30,775	1423
Rotation around the sun (years)	12 years	29.5 years	84 years	165 years	248 years
Orbital speed around sun	26.6 ft/s	19.6 ft/s	13.8 ft/s	10.26 ft/s	9.67 ft/s
Rotation time	9 h. 55 m.	10 h. 40 m.	17 h. 14 m.	16 h. 7 m.	6 days 9 h.
Mass (Earth = 1))	318	95.18	14.5	17.14	0.0022
Density (water = 1)	1.33	0.69	1.29	1.64	2.03
Temperature in high clouds (°F)	−234°	−288°	−353°	−353°	−369° to -387°
Number of moons	16	18	15	8	1

Uranus

At the limit of sight, this planet looks at first like just another star, barely visible on a clear night. With binoculars it is easy to spot. It is spherical, but flattened, with a brightness comparable to that of Jupiter and Saturn. It has a system of rings and a family of moons.

Saturn

Although Saturn is almost twice as far from Earth as Jupiter, its immense size makes it visible to the naked eye for ten months of the year. Its rings, however, can only be seen with definition at magnifications of 20-30 or more. Even more difficult is finding Titan, the only one of Saturn's 18 moons that is visible using binoculars.

Jupiter

Although Jupiter is quite far from us, the bright reflection of sunlight on its dense atmosphere makes it visible from the Earth ten months of the year. Jupiter's surface, however, is covered by clouds, and therefore is not visible. Through a medium-power telescope it can be seen that the planet has bands of different color running parallel to its equator. Jupiter has more than 17 moons. The two outermost moons, Ganymede and Callisto, are the easiest to find with binoculars.

Jupiter

Saturn

Mars

Venus

Mercury

At certain times of the year, and with a clear sky, Jupiter, Saturn, Mars, Venus and Mercury can all be seen in the same visual area.

Spying on the Star King

The sun is the star at the heart of our solar system, closest to the Earth. It therefore is the only star that can be observed in detail. That said, its observation requires extreme precaution, which makes it an unsuitable object for beginners.

The brightest in the sky

The sun is at an average distance of about 92,955,820.5 miles from the Earth, the average temperature of its surface is 9,932 °F, and the light it produces takes more than 8 minutes to reach us.

When to observe the sun?

The best moment is just after dawn, when the air has not yet been warmed by the heat of the sun and remains stable. Towards midday the sun is higher over the horizon, but atmospheric disturbances damage the quality of the image.

photosphere

this is the bright, luminous layer that we see from the Earth. Its yellow color follows from its high temperature of 9,932 °F.

sunspots

these are regions that are darker in color because their temperature is lower than the regions around them.

chromosphere

this is a layer that extends over the visible surface of the sun, the photosphere. It cannot be seen under normal conditions because of the feeble light that it emits. Consequently, it is only evident during eclipses of the sun.

protuberances

these are powerful, curved eruptions of hot gas. They can only be seen during a total eclipse of the sun.

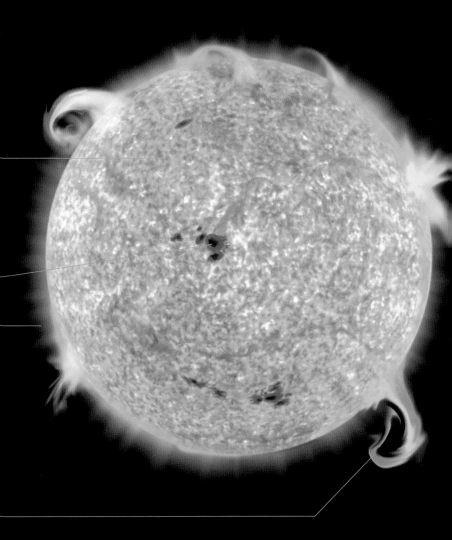

Spots in motion

Sunspots are continually changing in shape and size. They appear and disappear and move as solar rotation advances.

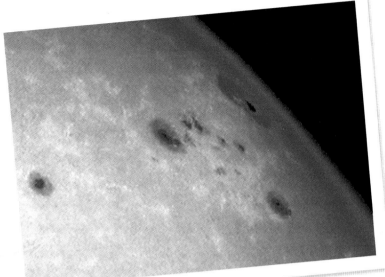

Methods of Observation

The filter

The most efficient and advisable method consists of a system that filters practically all the light of the sun. It involves putting an accessory on a telescope's light entry so that the optical system, particularly its eyepieces, does not overheat.

Projection

This method consists of projecting the sun's image directly from the eyepiece onto a flat, white surface. The further the projection surface is from the eyepiece, the larger the image will be. But it must be kept in mind that because light disperses, there is a limit to projection distance.

Caution!

You should never look directly at the sun, either with the naked eye or with an instrument. The light would burn the retina and could cause permanent blindness.

Even with specially approved glasses we should not look at the sun for more than 3 minutes at a stretch. When observing the sun, frequent breaks of at least 30 seconds are required.

Beautiful Selene

Called Selene by the Ancient Greeks and Luna in Latin, the moon is the first object at which the amateur in astronomy tends to aim his or her telescope, even though only one side of it can be seen from earth. The most important features to observe are the numerous impact craters and the great flat extensions of lava that are called seas.

When to observe the moon?

The best time for observation is not when the moon is full, but when it is in its first and last quarters and on the days around then. At full moon we cannot see the contours of the lunar landscape since the sun's rays hit the moon's surface perpendicularly, meaning that the formations on the surface do not cast shadows. Geographical features can be seen best along the terminator line as it moves across the moon's surface from one phase to the next.

The dark side

Since the moon's travel in its orbit around the Earth and its rotation on its own axis take approximately the same amount of time, the result is that the moon always shows the same part of its surface to the Earth, while its other side remains hidden from the Earth, impossible to view.

seas or maria

these are great dark lava plains that seem like seas when seen from the Earth.

craters

these were formed as a result of meteorites of different sizes hitting the moon's surface.

the terminator

the zone between the sunlit part and the dark part of the moon.

With the naked eye?

The moon can easily be observed with the naked eye, though with simple binoculars we will be better able to appreciate some of the geographical features on its surface. However, a telescope is necessary to clearly see its craters and seas.

The moon to the naked eye

The moon observed with binoculars

The moon seen through a home telescope.

The phases of the moon

Since the moon orbits around the Earth, the light of the sun reaches it from different positions, repeated in the course of each full cycle. When the entire side of the moon that we can see is lit by the sun, we have a full moon. When we cannot see the moon at all, we have a new moon. Between these two phases only a quarter of the moon can be seen, waxing or waning.

new moon

waxing moon

first quarter

waxing gibbous

full moon

waning gibbous

last quarter

waning moon

A specialized guidebook.

21

A Grand Spectacle

One of the most spectacular astronomical phenomena is an eclipse, the darkening of the sun or moon for a short period of time. Eclipses occur when the Earth, the moon and the sun are lined up and on the same orbital plane. When this happens and the Earth's shadow falls on the moon, an eclipse of the moon occurs. When the moon's shadow falls on the Earth, it's an eclipse of the sun. If one celestial body totally conceals the other, it is a total eclipse. Otherwise, it's a partial one.

eclipse of the moon
this happens when the moon passes through some part of the Earth's shadow.

eclipse of the sun
this happens when the moon is interposed between the Earth and the sun, and its shadow falls on part of our planet.

1. umbra or interior shadow
this is the darkest part of the shadow.

2. penumbra or exterior shadow
this is the lightest part of the shadow. It produces only a slight darkening of the moon.

3. umbra or interior shadow
the zone of the Earth that is completely darkened by the effect of the moon's shadow. Here the eclipse is total.

4. penumbra or exterior shadow
the zone of the Earth that is darkened by the effect of the moon's shadow. Here the eclipse is partial.

22

Sun

Partial eclipse of the sun

In the region that is in the penumbra (far more extensive than the umbra) observers will see that the moon only covers part of the solar disk.

An infrequent phenomenon

Eclipses are not all that frequent since the orbital plane of the moon and that of the sun are tilted 5°. If this were not the case, every month at full moon we would have a lunar eclipse and an eclipse of the sun at new moon.

The Earth is interposed between the sun and the moon without causing an eclipse of the moon: the moon passes behind the Earth but above its shadow, so an eclipse does not occur.

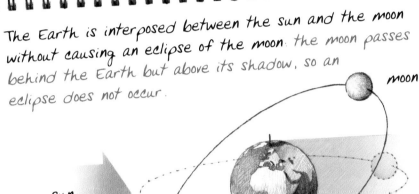

moon

sun

Earth

Total eclipse of the sun

Only observers on the part of the Earth that is passed over by the moon's umbra will see how completely it covers the solar disk.

Annular eclipse of the sun

This occurs when the moon does not completely cover the solar disk and a bright ring of light remains visible.

The moon passes between the sun and the Earth without causing an eclipse of the sun: the moon passes in front of the Earth but is not interposed between it and the sun since its orbit is tilted.

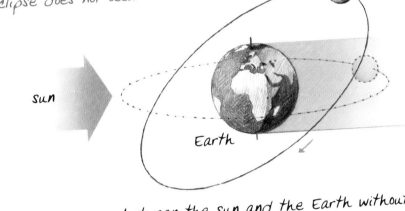

moon

sun

Earth

Figures in the Firmament

Ancient civilizations grouped the stars that were visible from Earth into recognizable forms they called constellations. These were given the names of mythological figures (Orion, Andromeda, Perseus, for example), or of animals and objects (Great Bear, Little Bear, Lion, Northern Crown, among others) depending on the character, animal or object suggested by the shape.

Groups of stars

Today, 88 constellations have been identified, many of which are visible from both hemispheres of the Earth, though some are observable only from one.

Circumpolar constellations

These are constellations that can be seen in the northern hemisphere, are visible all year round, are never hidden and never set.

Dragon

Cepheus

Little Bear

Cassiopeia

Great Bear

Spring constellations

In this season, unlike in the winter, we look out into deep space into a fainter portion of the sky that is quite free of stars and is called "the kingdom of the galaxies" by astronomers.

The Herdsman
The Hunting Dogs
Bernice's Hair
Northern Crown
The Crow
The Cup
The Dragon
The Hydra

The Lion

The Virgin

Summer constellations

Now the position of the Earth is such that we look toward the galactic center of the Milky Way, into a sky rich in stars and deep objects.

The Goat
The Dolphin
The Dragon
The Shield
The Arrow
Hercules
The Harp
The Serpent Bearer
The Archer
The Serpent

The Eagle

The Swan

The pole (north) star

Perhaps the most famous star in the North sky, this can be found if an imaginary extension of the Earth's axis in the northern hemisphere is followed into the celestial sphere. It belongs to the constellation of Ursa Minor (Little Bear). Before the invention of the compass, it was the only point of reference to indicate the north.

north star

Little Bear

North Pole

South Pole

Autumn constellations

By mid-autumn the night sky will have changed. Those crowded regions of the Milky Way so full of bright stars that made the sky in August so dense and rich give way to a dark emptiness. At this time, instead of looking toward the center of our galaxy, we are gazing outward into immense, intergalactic space.

The Water Carrier
The Ram
The Whale
Cassiopeia
Cepheus
The Giraffe
Pegasus
The Triangle

Andromeda

Perseus

The winter sky

It is truly splendid when the nights are calm and clear.

The Hare
The Little Dog
The Charioteer
The Bull
The Twins
The Unicorn

Orion

The Big Dog

More Fantastic Figures

In the southern sky marvels can be observed, such as the stars Rigel and Eta Carina; the famous Southern Cross constellation; globular clusters like Omega Centauri; galaxies like the two Clouds of Magellan; and nebulas such as the Coal Sack. If we focus on constellations alone, 49 of the 88 in existence are to be found between the ecliptic zone and the South Celestial Pole.

A pole without a pole star

There is no pole star in the southern hemisphere, but it is well worth observing the rich field of stars to be seen. These are constellations visible throughout the entire year by an observer situated in the southern hemisphere, but are invisible to those in the northern hemisphere.

Names old and new

While the names currently in use for the constellations of the northern hemisphere come from Greek mythology, those for the southern constellations are of more recent origin and are linked to the discoveries of sailors dating from the 17th century.

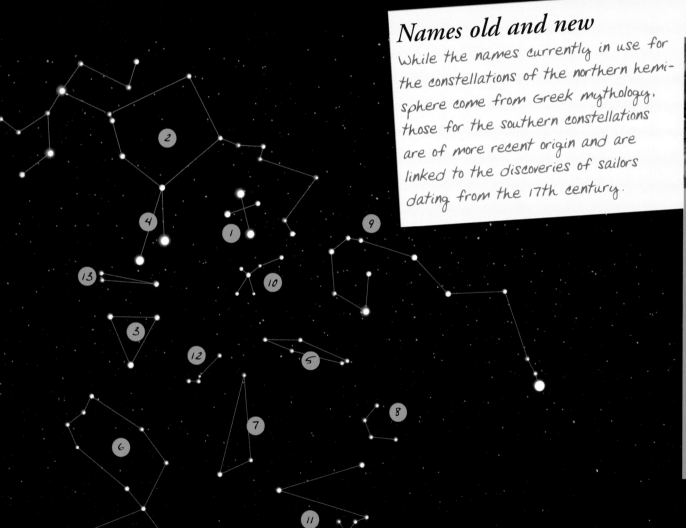

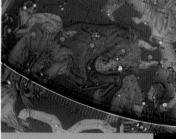

1. Southern Cross
2. The Centaur
3. Southern Triangle
4. The Compass
5. The Chameleon
6. The Peacock
7. The Octant
8. The Table
9. The Keel
10. The Fly
11. The Water Snake
12. Bird of Paradise
13. The Swordfish

The clouds of Magellan

These are two small galaxies, satellites of the Milky Way that are about 160,000 light years away and represent the external galaxies closest to us, just after Andromeda. They are easily observable by the naked eye from anywhere in the southern hemisphere (and at latitudes below 20° in the northern sky).

NGC 1850 • Star Clusters in the Large Mag
NASA, ESA and M. Romaniello (European Southern O

They are not so close

Constellations are not actually made up of neighboring stars. Although the stars belonging to a constellation may seem close to one another, in reality they are often hundreds of light years apart.

The Coal Sack

In the constellation of the Southern Cross, there is a big dark zone that is almost without stars and stands out against the background of the Milky Way. Known as the Coal Sack, it can be seen by the unassisted eye.

The globular cluster Omega Centauri

Globular clusters are groupings of very old stars that are found circling the galaxies. Omega Centauri contains some 10 million stars and is the southern hemisphere's brightest cluster. It appears to the naked eye as a small fluffy spot.

The Rascals of Space

Apart from stars, planets and the moon, on occasion
the night sky offers us an even more fantastic spectacle,
where the leading actors are marvelous meteoroids,
otherwise known as shooting or falling stars,
mysterious comets, fireballs and fearsome meteorites.

meteor or shooting star
the luminous phenomenon
or flash of light that
occurs when a meteoroid,
attracted by the gravity
of the Earth, burns up
and disintegrates on
contact with the Earth's
atmosphere.

meteoroid
a fragment of matter
traveling through
interplanetary space.

Where do comets come from?
They come chiefly from two
places: the Kuiper Belt, located
beyond the orbit of the planet
Pluto, and from the Oort Cloud,
even further away, halfway
between Earth and Alpha
Centauri (the star closest to
the sun).

28

comet
a asteroid-like object
that orbits around the
sun and is
characterized by the
long, bright tail that
appears when it passes
close to the sun.

meteorite
a meteoroid that
manages to reach the
Earth's surface.

The passage of a comet portrayed in the famous Bayeux Tapestry (11th century).

Asteroids have crashed into our planet in the distant past. One of the best-preserved examples is the Barringer Crater in Arizona, produced, it is thought, by the impact of a piece of an asteroid 50,000 years ago. It is around 4,000 feet in diameter and 570 feet deep.

Asteroids

These are rocky objects that orbit around the Sun but that are too small to be considered planets. Their size varies, from those with a diameter of around 600 miles to others that are the size of a large rock. They have been found in different places, though most of them are in the largest asteroid belt between the orbits of Mars and Jupiter.

Parts of a comet

Fireballs

These are meteoroids that are larger than those that create shooting stars and for that reason the light they release is of particular intensity and brightness.

fuzzy head or coma
when a comet gets close to the sun a cloud of gas and dust forms around it.

nucleus
its solid part, made up of ice, organic compounds, dust and other frozen substances.

ion tail
produced by the interaction between a solar wind and a comet

hydrogen envelope
this cannot be seen from Earth since its light is absorbed by our atmosphere.

dust tail
when a comet gets close to the sun, it forms a bright tail that in general stretches away from the sun.

Scanning the Universe

An astronomical observatory is made up of equipment designed to pick up all sorts of electromagnetic waves, thereby allowing for the study of the celestial bodies and galaxies of the universe. Astronomical observatories are equipped with powerful telescopes, capable of detecting different waves coming from way out in space, millions of light years from the Earth.

observation opening

this consists of two sliding shutters, one above, larger in size, that retracts into the back part of the dome, and another, smaller one that slides into the front part.

dome of aluminum-coated iron

the dome is air-conditioned during the day and heat-insulated in order to maintain the telescope chamber at a proper nighttime temperature.

annex building

this building houses auxiliary and support services for the installation, such as the control room, storerooms and maintenance workshops.

Solar telescope

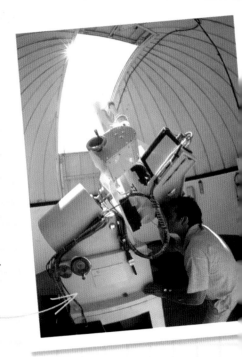

This telescope is designed to measure the intensity and direction of the solar magnetic field. It makes it possible for researchers to see and photograph the smallest details of the sun's surface.

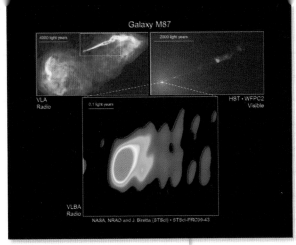

Galaxy M87

Observing very distant objects

In astronomy, objects of study are so far away that distances are measured in light years (the distance light travels in a year at a speed of 186,000 meters per second, or 5,880,000,000,000 miles).

Looking for high ground

Astronomical observatories on Earth are built at high altitudes to avoid the light pollution produced by cities and to reduce the absorption of electromagnetic radiation from the atmosphere as much as possible.

31

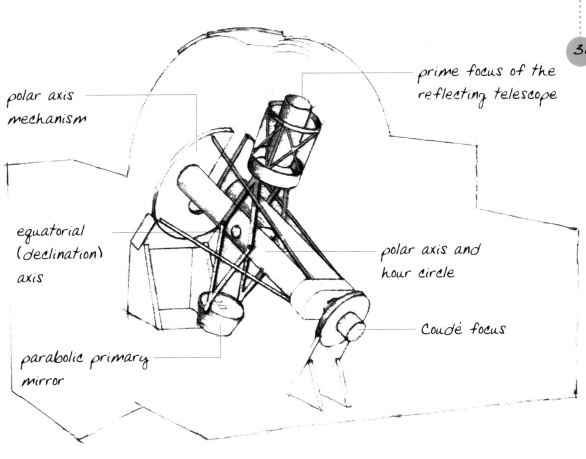

polar axis mechanism

prime focus of the reflecting telescope

equatorial (declination) axis

polar axis and hour circle

Coudé focus

parabolic primary mirror

32

Some nebulas

Name	Constellation	Approximate distance (light years)
NGC 3372 (Eta Carinae)	Keel	3.700
NGC 2070 (Tarántula)	Swordfish	180.000
M 57 (Ring)	Harp	5.000
NGC 2237 (Rosette)	Unicorn	3.000
M 42 (Great Nebula)	Orión	1.500
M 8 (Lagoon)	Archer	4.500
M 17 (Omega)	Archer	5.500
M 20 (Trifid)	Archer	3.500
M 1 (Crab)	Bull	4.000
M 27	Fox	3.500

Some galaxies

Name	Constellation	Type	Approximate distance (millions of light years)
M 31	Andromeda	Spiral	2,3
NGC 5128	Centaur	Elliptical	13
Large Cloud of Magellan	Swordfish	Irregular	0,17
NGC 253	Sculptor	Spiral	10
M 33	Triangle	Spiral	2,3
Small Cloud of Magellan	Toucan	Irregular	0,20
M 81	Great Bear	Spiral	7
M 87	Virgin	Elliptical	40
M 104	Virgin	Spiral	40

The ten closest stars

Name	Constellation	Distance (light years)
Próxima Centauri	Centaur	4,24
Alpha Centauri	Centaur	4,37
Barnard's Star	Ophiuchus	6,0
Wolf 359	Lion	7,8
Lalande 21185	Great Bear	8,2
Luyten 726-8	Whale	8,5
Sirius	Big Dog	8,6
Ross 154	Archer	9,6
Ross 248	Andromeda	10,3
Epsilon Eridani	Eridanus	10,6

Major annual meteor showers

Shower	Date*	Frequency per hour	Parent comet
Quadrantids	3 January	40	Asteroid 2003 EH
Lyrids	22 April	15	Comet Thatcher
Eta Aquarids	5 May	20	Halley's Comet
Delta Aquarids	28 July	20	(Not known)
Perseids	12 August	50	Swift-Tuttle Comet
Orionids	22 October	25	Halley's Comet
Taurids	3 November	15	Encke's Comet
Leonids	17 November	13	Temple-Tuttle Comet
Geminids	14 December	50	Asteroid 3200 Phaethon
Ursids	23 December	20	Tuttle Comet

*The dates indicated correspond to the days of greatest frequency and can vary slightly from year to year.

Index

Alpha Centauri (star) 13, 32
Andromeda (constellation) 25, 27
annular (eclipse of the sun) 23
asteroids, 29
astronomical observatory 30-31
astronomy, where to find out more? 5
autumn (constellations) 25
azimuth mounting (telescope) 7

Barnard's Star 32
barred spiral (galaxy) 11
Barringer Crater (US) 29
Big Dog (constellation) 25
binoculars, 4, 5
Bird of Paradise, The (constellation) 26
brightness (of the stars) 13

Cassiopeia (constellation) 24
celestial sphere 9
Cepheus (constellation) 24
Centaur (constellation) 13, 26, 32
Chameleon (constellation) 26
chromosphere (sun) 18
circular scale (planisphere) 8
circumpolar (constellations) 24
Clouds of Magellan 27, 32
Coal Sack 27
coma (of comet) 29
comets 28-29
compass, 4
Compass (constellation) 26
constellations 24-27
Coudé focus (telescope) 31

dark side of the moon 20
Dragon (constellation) 24
dust tail (of comet) 29

Eagle (constellation) 24
Earth 15
eclipses 22-23
elliptical (galaxy) 11
Epsilon Eridani (star) 32
equatorial mounting (telescope) 7
equatorial axis (telescope) 31
Eta Aquarids (meteors) 32
eyepiece (telescope) 6
exterior shadow (eclipse) 22

first quarter (moon) 21
flashlight 4, 5
Fly (constellation) 26
full moon 21
fuzzy head (of comet) 29

galactic center 10
galactic disk 10
galactic halo 10, 11
galaxies 10-11, 32
Geminids (meteors) 32
globular clusters 11
Great Bear (constellation) 24

Hydra (constellation) 26
hydrogen (of comet) 29
hydrogen envelope (of comet) 29

interior shadow (eclipse) 22
ion tail (of comet) 29
irregular galaxy 11

Jovian planets 16-17
Jupiter 16, 17

Keel (constellation) 26

Lalande 21185 (star) 32
last quarter (moon) 21
Leonids (meteors) 32
Lion (constellation) 24
Little Bear (constellation) 24
lunar craters 20, 21
Luyten 726-8 (star) 32
Lyrids (meteors) 32

Magellan, Clouds of 27, 32
Mars 14, 15
Mercury 14, 15
meteorites 28-29
meteoroids 27-28
meteors 28, 29
meteor showers 32
Milky Way 8, 10, 27

moon 20-21, 22, 23
moon, dark side of 20
multiple stars 12

nebulas 11, 32
Neptune 16
neutron star 12
new moon 21
north star 25
northern hemisphere 9, 24-25
notebook for observation 4, 5
nucleus (of comet) 29

objective (telescope) 6
observation opening 30
observatory dome 30
Octant (constellation) 26
Omega Centauri (cluster) 27
open clusters 11
Orion (constellation)
Orionids (meteors) 32

partial eclipse of the sun 23
Peacock (constellation) 26
penumbra (eclipse) 22
Perseids (meteors) 32
Perseus (constellation) 25
phases of the moon 21
photosphere (sun) 18
planisphere 4, 5, 8-9
Pluto 16
polar axis (telescope) 31
pole star 25
primary mirror (telescope) 31
prime focus (telescope) 31
projection of the hemispheres 9
protuberances (sun) 18
Proxima Centauri (star) 32

Quadrantids (meteors) 32

red dwarf (star) 12
reflected light (telescope) 6
refracted light (telescope) 6
reflector telescope 6
refractor telescope 6
rings (of Saturn) 17
Ross 154 (star) 32
Ross 248 (star) 32

Saturn 16, 17
seas or maria (moon) 20

secondary reflector (telescope) 6
Selene (star) 20
shooting stars 28
Sirius (star) 32
sky, exploring 4-5
solar filter 19
solar projection
solar system 10, 15
solar telescope 30
Southern Cross (constellation) 26
southern hemisphere 9, 26-27
Southern Triangle (constellation) 26
spiral arms, 10
spiral galaxy 11
spring constellations 24
star atlas 5
stars 12-13, 32
summer constellations 24
sun 18-19, 22, 23
sunglasses 19
sunspots 18, 19
supernova 12
Swan (constellation) 24
Swordfish (constellation) 26

Table (constellation) 26
Taurids (meteors) 32
terminator (moon) 20
terrestrial planets 14-15
total eclipse of the sun 23

umbra (eclipse) 22
Uranus 16, 17
Ursids (meteors) 32

Venus 14, 15
Venus Express (probe) 14
viewfinder (telescope) 6, 7
Virgin (constellation) 24

waning gibbous (moon) 21
waning moon 21
waxing gibbous (moon) 21
waxing moon 21
white dwarf (star) 12
winter (constellations) 25
Wolf 359 (star) 32

What Do We Need to Observe the Sky?

A nighttime expedition to observe the sky can be truly exciting. This guide will help make your expedition a success by indicating what can be observed with available instruments, along with the ideal conditions for observing each phenomenon. With patience and a great deal of attention it is possible to see a truly wonderful live show.

With a good pair of **binoculars** it is possible to see details such as lunar craters and mountains; the planets and some of their satellites; the brightest asteroids; some comets; innumerable double and variable stars; dozens of star clusters; some nebulas and galaxies; and the center of our galaxy and the Milky Way.

To enjoy astronomic observation it is not necessary to have the latest model **telescope**. Rather, what is important is to have one that serves its purpose well. Therefore, it is necessary to have a sturdy, stable tripod that can support the entire instrument without bending or vibrations. If it fails to do its job, everything on top of it will fail as well. It should have a solid frame, with very gentle movement, and on top of the frame a tube with optics in which quality prevails over diameter. Finally, it should have two or three good eyepieces (quality over quantity.)